Linkedin Marketing

How to Amplify Your Business and Generate Organic Leads with Sales Navigator

Joel Erlichson

© 2023 by Joel Erlichson.
All rights reserved.

No part of this book may be reproduced in any form or by any electronic or mechanical means, including information storage and retrieval systems, without written permission from the author, except for the use of brief quotations in a book review.

Table Of Contents

Introduction

- The Power of LinkedIn Marketing
- Understanding LinkedIn Sales Navigator

Chapter 1: The Essentials of LinkedIn Marketing

- The Benefits of LinkedIn for Business
- LinkedIn vs. Other Social Media Platforms
- Creating a Compelling LinkedIn Profile

Chapter 2: LinkedIn Sales Navigator Basics

- Overview of Sales Navigator Features
- Setting Up Your Sales Navigator Account
- Understanding the Sales Navigator Interface

Chapter 3: Lead Generation with Sales Navigator

- LeadBuilder: Your Tool for Quality Leads
- Saving and Monitoring Key Prospects and Accounts
- Advanced Search Techniques

Chapter 4: Maximizing the Power of TeamLink

- Understanding TeamLink Connections
- Leveraging TeamLink for Warm Leads

Chapter 5: Account Mapping and Documentation

- Using Lucidchart for Account Mapping
- Documenting Findings and Insights
- Organizing Prospects with Tags and Notes

Chapter 6: Broadening Your Prospects

- Identifying Similar Prospects
- Extending Your Reach Beyond Initial Search Criteria

Chapter 7: Advanced Search Features

- Advanced Filters and Their Benefits
- Discovering Untapped Connections

Chapter 8: Building Rapport through Shared Experiences

- The Power of Shared Experiences in Sales
- Utilizing the "Shared Experiences" Filter

Chapter 9: LinkedIn Profile Optimization

- The Importance of a Well-Crafted Profile
- Key Elements of an Effective LinkedIn Profile

Chapter 10: Social Selling and Success with Sales Navigator

- The Impact of Social Selling
- Using Sales Navigator to Increase Win Rates and Deal Sizes

Conclusion

- The Future of LinkedIn Marketing and Sales Navigator
- Staying Updated with LinkedIn's Changes and Enhancements

Introduction

Welcome to "LinkedIn Marketing: How To Amplify Your Business and Generate Organic Leads with Sales Navigator". If you're a business person looking to optimize your LinkedIn presence and leverage this powerful platform to grow your business, then you're in the right place.

LinkedIn has revolutionized the way professionals connect, interact, and do business. With over 700 million users, it's not just a network; it's a goldmine of opportunities. But how can you, as a business professional, tap into this network and turn connections into fruitful business relationships? This is precisely what this guide aims to help you achieve.

We understand that marketing, especially on a platform as vast as LinkedIn, can seem overwhelming if it's not your background. Therefore, this book has been designed with you in mind. We break down the complexities of LinkedIn marketing into manageable, easy-to-understand sections. Whether you're entirely new to LinkedIn or have been using it passively, this book will equip you with the knowledge and skills to become a LinkedIn marketing pro.

We'll begin by exploring the basics of LinkedIn and its unique advantages for business. From there, we'll dive into the LinkedIn Sales Navigator tool, an advanced feature that takes lead generation and customer acquisition to a whole new level.

You'll learn how to use Sales Navigator to create a solid pipeline, identify quality leads, and significantly improve your sales prospecting.

The book also covers advanced techniques, such as leveraging TeamLink connections, creating account maps, and using advanced search features for optimal results. Plus, we'll guide you through the process of optimizing your LinkedIn profile to make a stellar first impression on prospects.

By the end of this guide, you'll have the tools, knowledge, and confidence to harness the full potential of LinkedIn.

You'll be able to transform your LinkedIn profile from a simple online resume into a powerful business tool that generates organic leads, builds meaningful relationships, and boosts your business.

It's time to unlock the power of LinkedIn and take your business to the next level. Let's begin this exciting journey towards LinkedIn marketing mastery.

Chapter 1: The Essentials of LinkedIn Marketing

The Benefits of LinkedIn for Business

In the world of business, the importance of a robust online presence cannot be overstated. Among the multitude of online platforms available, LinkedIn stands out as a vital tool for any business looking to build a strong professional network, attract potential clients, and grow its brand. Here are some of the key benefits of LinkedIn for business:

- **Access to a Massive Professional Network:** LinkedIn is the world's largest professional networking platform, with over 700 million users spanning various industries worldwide.

This massive audience presents businesses with unlimited opportunities to connect with potential clients, partners, and industry influencers.

- **Enhanced Credibility:** A well-optimized LinkedIn profile can significantly enhance your business's credibility. It provides an excellent platform to showcase your business's achievements, expertise, and offerings. Plus, LinkedIn allows for customer testimonials, endorsements, and recommendations, further boosting your credibility.

- **Lead Generation and Customer Acquisition:** LinkedIn is a powerhouse for lead generation.

According to data from HubSpot, LinkedIn is 277% more effective for lead generation than Facebook or Twitter. It provides a platform where businesses can share valuable content, engage with potential clients, and ultimately convert those leads into customers.

- **Valuable Industry Insights:** LinkedIn is a valuable source of industry news and trends. By following industry influencers and joining relevant groups, businesses can stay updated on the latest happenings in their industry, giving them a competitive edge.

- **Humanizing Your Brand:** LinkedIn provides businesses with a unique opportunity to humanize their brand.

You can share behind-the-scenes looks at your company, celebrate employee achievements, and engage with followers in a more personal way. This fosters stronger relationships and builds trust with your audience.

- **B2B Marketing Powerhouse:** If your business is B2B (Business to Business), LinkedIn is arguably the most effective platform for marketing. It offers various tools and features specifically designed for B2B marketing, such as Sales Navigator, which we will explore in greater detail later in this guide.

- **Talent Acquisition:** LinkedIn is also a fantastic tool for attracting top talent to your company.

By showcasing your company culture and values, and posting job opportunities, you can attract high-quality candidates who can drive your business forward.

As we delve deeper into this guide, we'll explore how to leverage these benefits and utilize LinkedIn's features to amplify your business. From creating a compelling profile to effectively utilizing Sales Navigator, you'll learn how to make LinkedIn a powerful tool for your business's growth and success.

LinkedIn vs. Other Social Media Platforms

While LinkedIn is considered a social media platform, it differs significantly from other popular platforms like Facebook, Instagram, or Twitter. The primary difference lies in the purpose of the platform: LinkedIn is a professional networking site, while the others are predominantly used for personal socializing, entertainment, or casual interaction.

LinkedIn's professional focus offers businesses a unique opportunity to connect with other businesses, potential clients, and industry influencers in a professional setting. Content shared on LinkedIn is typically more formal and business-oriented. It is a place to share industry insights, business achievements, and professional news.

On the other hand, platforms like Facebook and Instagram are often used for more informal, personal interactions. These platforms are excellent for showcasing the personality of your business, behind-the-scenes glimpses, or more casual, fun content.

Each platform has its unique strengths and can serve different aspects of your business marketing strategy. However, for professional networking, B2B marketing, and lead generation, LinkedIn often comes out on top.

Creating a Compelling LinkedIn Profile

A compelling LinkedIn profile serves as your virtual business card and is often the first point of contact for potential clients or partners on LinkedIn.

It can significantly influence the impression you make on your LinkedIn audience. Here are some key steps to creating a compelling LinkedIn profile:

1. Professional Photo: Start with a high-quality, professional headshot. This is the first thing people see on your profile, and it can significantly impact their first impression.

2. Compelling Headline: Your headline should be concise, clear, and reflect your business's value proposition. It is often displayed in LinkedIn search results, so make sure it effectively represents you and your business.

3. Detailed Summary: The summary section is your opportunity to tell your business's story. Highlight your offerings, achievements, values, and what sets you apart from your competition. Make it engaging and relevant to your target audience.

4. Showcase Your Experience: Include detailed information about your business experience, roles, and achievements. Don't forget to highlight key projects or significant milestones.

5. Recommendations and Endorsements: Recommendations and endorsements from clients or colleagues can significantly boost your credibility. Don't hesitate to ask for them.

6. Regular Updates: Keep your profile updated with your latest business achievements, projects, or changes. An up-to-date profile shows that you are active and engaged on the platform.

Remember, a compelling LinkedIn profile isn't just about listing your business information. It's about presenting your business in a way that resonates with your target audience and positions you as a reliable, credible choice in your industry.

Chapter 2: LinkedIn Sales Navigator Basics

If you're looking to take your LinkedIn marketing to the next level, LinkedIn Sales Navigator is a tool you absolutely need to become familiar with. Sales Navigator is an advanced LinkedIn tool designed to enhance lead generation and sales prospecting. It helps you find the right people, stay up-to-date with them, and understand your accounts better. Let's delve into the basics.

Overview of Sales Navigator Features

Sales Navigator comes packed with features that can significantly enhance your marketing efforts. Some of the key features include:

- **Lead Recommendations:** Sales Navigator provides personalized lead recommendations based on your sales preferences and search history.

- **Advanced Search:** With over 20 advanced search filters, you can find the right leads and accounts faster.

- **InMail:** You can send direct messages to any LinkedIn member, even if you're not connected.

- **Real-time Sales Updates:** Get real-time updates on your saved leads and accounts, such as job changes and company updates.

- **Lead and Account Saving:** You can save leads and accounts, and Sales Navigator will provide updates and recommend similar leads.

- **TeamLink Connections:** This feature lets you see who in your company knows your saved leads, helping you get warm introductions.

- **CRM Integration:** Sales Navigator integrates with various CRM platforms, making it easier to manage and track your activities.

Setting Up Your Sales Navigator Account

Setting up your Sales Navigator account is quite straightforward. Follow these steps:

- Start by going to the LinkedIn Sales Navigator page and click on 'Start my free trial' if you want to test it out before purchasing a plan.

- After the trial period, you can choose the plan that suits your needs. LinkedIn offers Professional, Team, and Enterprise Sales Navigator plans.

- After selecting a plan, you'll be prompted to set up your Sales Navigator account. This involves defining your sales preferences, such as the industries, company sizes, and job functions you're targeting.

- Import your contacts from your CRM or add them manually.

Remember to review your sales preferences regularly and adjust them as your business needs evolve.

Understanding the Sales Navigator Interface

The Sales Navigator interface might seem a bit overwhelming at first, but it's relatively straightforward once you understand its layout. Here's a quick rundown:

- **Home:** This is your Sales Navigator homepage. Here you'll see updates from your saved leads and accounts.

- **Search Bar:** Use this to search for leads or accounts. You can use the advanced search filters to refine your results.

- My Lists: Here you can access your saved leads and accounts.

- Messages: This is where you can access your InMail messages.

- Alerts: Here, you'll receive alerts about job changes, leads who have posted on LinkedIn recently, and more.

- Learning Center: If you need help, the Learning Center provides useful resources and tutorials.

- Admin: If you're an administrator, you can access your Sales Navigator management tools here.

By understanding these basics, you're already on your way to becoming a proficient Sales Navigator user. In the following chapters, we'll dive deeper into how you can leverage these features to amplify your business and generate organic leads on LinkedIn. Remember, mastery comes with practice, so don't hesitate to explore and experiment with the features as you go.

Chapter 3: Lead Generation with Sales Navigator

LinkedIn Sales Navigator is designed to streamline and enhance the process of finding, connecting, and engaging with prospects. In this chapter, we'll delve into the platform's powerful lead generation capabilities.

LeadBuilder: Your Tool for Quality Leads

At the heart of Sales Navigator's lead generation capabilities is a feature known as LeadBuilder. LeadBuilder is a highly effective tool that allows you to develop a highly targeted and relevant pipeline of leads.

To use LeadBuilder, navigate to the search bar and click on the "LeadBuilder" button. You'll be directed to an advanced search page where you can choose from over 20 filters to target the types of leads you're looking for. These filters include company, job title, industry, company size, and geography.

Remember, the quality of your leads is more important than the quantity. So be as specific as you can with your search filters to ensure the leads you're targeting are the most relevant to your business.

Saving and Monitoring Key Prospects and Accounts

Once you've conducted your search, Sales Navigator allows you to save all relevant prospects in the search results to build your list. To save a prospect, simply click the 'save' button next to their name in the search results.

Sales Navigator will then populate those leads in your newsfeed so you can monitor any updates or changes at a glance. This could include job changes, recent activity, or company updates, helping you keep your finger on the pulse without having to manually check each lead's profile.

A pro tip here is to also save your searches. This feature sends you notifications when new prospects matching your criteria show up in the system, so you're always up to date with potential leads.

Advanced Search Techniques:
Sales Navigator's advanced search feature is a powerful tool that allows you to discover new leads based on very specific criteria. Some of the advanced search features you can utilize include:

Lead Recommendations: Sales Navigator will provide recommendations for leads based on your saved leads and search history.

Posting Activity: You can filter your search to show leads that have posted on LinkedIn in the past 30 days.

Company Connections: Discover who in your network is connected to a specific company.

News Mention: Find leads who have been mentioned in the news recently, which can be a great conversation starter.

Shared Experiences: Use the 'Shared experiences with you' filter to find leads with whom you have something in common, making it easier to build rapport.

Job Changes: Identify leads who have recently changed jobs. This might indicate they're open to new opportunities or solutions.

These techniques can be highly effective in finding leads that are the most relevant to your business, improving your chances of success in your outreach efforts.

Remember, lead generation is not a one-size-fits-all process. It's crucial to continuously refine and adapt your approach based on what works best for your business and target audience. The more you use Sales Navigator and its features, the more you'll understand how to leverage them for maximum effect.

Chapter 4: Maximizing the Power of TeamLink

One of the most unique and powerful features of LinkedIn Sales Navigator is TeamLink. TeamLink is a networking tool that allows you to leverage your company's collective network to find the best path to a lead. This chapter will guide you on how to fully utilize this feature.

Understanding TeamLink Connections

The basic idea behind TeamLink is simple: it extends your network to include your colleagues' connections. This means that if you're connected to a colleague, and that colleague is connected to a prospect you're interested in, TeamLink will show that connection.

To access TeamLink, head over to your Sales Navigator homepage and find the 'TeamLink Connections' filter on the right side of your search bar. Here, you can see all of your TeamLink Connections at a glance.

One important thing to note is that TeamLink Connections only show shared connections up to the second degree. This means that if a connection is a third degree connection or further, they won't appear in your TeamLink Connections.

Leveraging TeamLink for Warm Leads

So, how can you use TeamLink to generate warm leads and improve your sales prospecting? Here are a few strategies:

Identify Shared Connections: Use the TeamLink Connections filter to identify prospects who have a shared connection with you. This can help you establish credibility and build rapport with prospects more quickly.

Leverage Your Colleague's Network: If a colleague is connected with a prospect, they can potentially introduce you, turning a cold lead into a warm one.

Save Your Searches: Don't forget to save your searches. If a new connection appears that matches your criteria, Sales Navigator will notify you.

Use on Account Pages: TeamLink also appears on account pages to show you which employees in a targeted company you might be connected to.

This can help you identify potential pathways into a target company.

Enhance Your InMail Strategy: Use TeamLink to mention shared connections in your InMail messages. This can help to personalize your messages and improve response rates.

Remember, networking is a powerful sales tool, and TeamLink is designed to help you make the most of your collective network. By understanding and leveraging TeamLink, you can find the best path to your prospects and significantly improve your LinkedIn marketing efforts.

Chapter 5: Account Mapping and Documentation

Even with the best tools at your disposal, effectively managing your leads and accounts can be challenging. This is especially true when you're dealing with a large volume of prospects and a variety of data points. This chapter will guide you on how to use account mapping and documentation to manage your leads effectively and make informed decisions.

Using Lucidchart for Account Mapping

Lucidchart is a visual workspace that can integrate with LinkedIn Sales Navigator to create a visual representation of your pipeline - this is known as account mapping.

This process can help you discover insights, make connections, and ultimately identify the quickest path to sale.

To start creating an account map, you'll first need to integrate Lucidchart with your LinkedIn Sales Navigator. Once integrated, you can start adding the contact information you discover in LinkedIn Sales Navigator to your account map.

The benefit of this visual layout is that it provides a clear view of your pipeline, showing how various leads and accounts are connected. This can help you identify potential opportunities, track your progress with each account, and prioritize your efforts.

Documenting Findings and Insights

The ability to document your findings directly within LinkedIn Sales Navigator is an incredibly valuable feature, especially when dealing with multiple prospects. You can jot down important information about a lead or account such as their pain points, interests, communication preferences, and any interactions you've had with them.

To add notes to a lead or account, simply navigate to their profile, scroll down to the 'Notes & Tags' section, and click 'Add note'. Here, you can enter any information you want to remember or share with your team.

Remember, these notes are visible to all Sales Navigator users in your organization, making it easy to collaborate and share insights with your team.

Organizing Prospects with Tags and Notes

In addition to notes, LinkedIn Sales Navigator allows you to categorize your leads and accounts using tags. Tags are customizable labels that you can apply to any lead or account.

For example, you might tag leads based on their industry, job role, where they are in the sales funnel, or any other criteria that's relevant to your sales process.

To add a tag, navigate to the lead or account's profile, scroll down to the 'Notes & Tags' section, and click 'Add tag'.

Tags provide a quick and easy way to segment your leads and accounts, making it easier to manage your pipeline and tailor your outreach efforts.

Proper account mapping and documentation is essential for managing your leads effectively, keeping track of important details, and making informed decisions. By utilizing these features in LinkedIn Sales Navigator, you can keep your pipeline organized and ensure you're always on top of your game.

Chapter 6: Broadening Your Prospects

Sales Navigator is not just about managing the leads you already know; it's also about discovering new potential leads. In this chapter, we'll delve into how you can broaden your prospect base by identifying similar prospects and extending your reach beyond your initial search criteria.

Identifying Similar Prospects

One of the powerful features of LinkedIn Sales Navigator is its ability to suggest similar prospects.

This is a quick and efficient way to expand your list of potential leads. As you use the Sales Navigator search functions to identify leads, you'll notice a drop-down button on a lead you're interested in. By selecting "View similar," you'll see a list of leads with similar job titles, roles, or industries from other companies.

This feature allows you to explore other potential leads that you might have otherwise overlooked. These leads are 'similar' based on the criteria you initially searched for, meaning they are highly relevant and likely to be of interest to you.

Extending Your Reach Beyond Initial Search Criteria

While Sales Navigator's advanced search features allow you to search for leads based on specific criteria, there's a lot of potential in looking beyond these initial parameters. Here are a few ways you can extend your reach:

Explore Other Industries or Job Titles: If you've been focusing on a specific industry or job title, consider expanding your search to include related industries or job titles.

Utilize Shared Experiences: Sales Navigator has a unique "Shared Experiences with You" filter that shows you leads who have something in common with you. This could be a past company, school, or group. These shared experiences can serve as an ice breaker and help to build rapport with new leads.

Look at Recent Activities: The Sales Navigator search function allows you to see who has posted on LinkedIn recently, who has been mentioned in the news, and who has changed jobs. This information can provide valuable context and open the door to new opportunities.

Leverage Your Existing Network: Use the TeamLink feature to see if any of your existing connections can introduce you to new leads.

By broadening your prospect search, you increase the opportunities to connect with potential leads that may have been overlooked. Remember, successful LinkedIn marketing involves a mix of targeted searches and exploration of new avenues. As you continue to use Sales Navigator, you'll likely find your own strategies for broadening your prospects and finding new leads.

Chapter 7: Advanced Search Features

The LinkedIn Sales Navigator offers a plethora of advanced search features, which when used effectively, can transform your lead generation and prospecting strategy. Let's delve into these features and how they can help you discover new, untapped connections.

Advanced Filters and Their Benefits

LinkedIn Sales Navigator provides numerous advanced filters that allow you to narrow down your search for leads or accounts. Here are some of the most valuable filters and their benefits:

- **Industry and Geography:** These filters allow you to target leads in specific industries or locations, which is particularly useful if your business offers industry-specific solutions or if you're targeting specific regional markets.

- **Company Headcount:** This filter can help you identify leads from small, mid-sized, or large companies based on your business's target market.

- **Seniority Level:** If you're looking to connect with decision-makers, this filter can help you find leads at the executive level.

- **Function:** This filter helps you find leads within specific departments of a company, such as marketing, sales, or human resources.

- **Changed Jobs in the Last 90 days:** This filter can help you identify leads who have recently changed jobs and might be open to new solutions or partnerships.

- **Leads that follow your company:** This filter shows leads who are already familiar with your brand and may be more open to your outreach efforts.

- **Posted on LinkedIn in the past 30 days:** This filter helps you identify active users on the platform, suggesting they might be more responsive to your messages.

Discovering Untapped Connections

One of the significant benefits of Sales Navigator's advanced search features is their ability to help you discover untapped connections. These are potential leads that you haven't yet connected with or may not have considered in your initial prospecting efforts. Here are some strategies to discover these connections:

- **Shared Connections:** The 'Shared Connections' filter shows you leads that have mutual connections with you. These mutual connections can serve as a bridge to new leads and potentially warm introductions.

- **Similar Prospects:** As mentioned in the previous chapter, the 'View similar' feature suggests prospects similar to a lead you're interested in. This can expose you to a wider range of potential leads that fit your target profile.

- **TeamLink Connections:** This feature shows leads that share a connection with your teammates. TeamLink can unveil a network of potential leads that you may not have access to individually.

By harnessing the power of Sales Navigator's advanced search features and exploring untapped connections, you can significantly expand your prospecting efforts and increase your opportunities for successful outreach.

Chapter 8: Building Rapport through Shared Experiences

In sales, building rapport with your prospects is crucial. It lays the foundation for trust, which can significantly affect your success in establishing a business relationship. One effective way to build rapport is through shared experiences, and LinkedIn Sales Navigator has a unique feature designed to help you identify these commonalities.

The Power of Shared Experiences in Sales

Shared experiences create a common ground, which can make your initial outreach more personalized and effective.

These shared experiences can serve as effective conversation starters, helping you break the ice and making your communication more personal. A personalized approach can make your prospect feel more comfortable and more open to what you have to say, as it shows that you took the time to understand them better.

Utilizing the "Shared Experiences" Filter

LinkedIn Sales Navigator has a "Shared Experiences with You" filter that shows you leads who have something in common with you. Here's how you can utilize this feature:

- **Filter your Search:** During your lead search, apply the "Shared Experiences with You" filter. This will narrow down your results to those who share some common ground with you.

- **Review Shared Experiences:** When you click on a prospect's profile, you can see a "Highlights" section that outlines what you have in common. This could include mutual connections, groups, schools, or past companies.

- **Personalize Your Outreach:** Use these shared experiences to personalize your outreach. You could mention the shared experience in your initial message to the prospect, which can serve as a great conversation opener.

Remember, the goal of leveraging shared experiences is not just to create an initial connection but to build meaningful relationships with your prospects. It's about using these shared experiences as a stepping stone to more in-depth, productive conversations about how your product or service can meet their needs.

In the next chapter, we'll explore how to optimize your LinkedIn profile to make a positive first impression on your leads. So stay tuned!

Chapter 9: LinkedIn Profile Optimization

Your LinkedIn profile is often the first point of contact between you and potential prospects. It serves as your online business card, your resume, and your personal branding platform all at once. Therefore, having a well-crafted, professional profile is of paramount importance.

The Importance of a Well-Crafted Profile

A compelling LinkedIn profile can help you:

- Stand out: With millions of users on LinkedIn, a well-crafted profile can help you stand out from the crowd.

- **Build credibility:** A complete, professional-looking profile lends credibility to you and your business.

- **Attract more leads:** A profile that clearly communicates your value proposition can attract more and better-qualified leads.

- **Increase visibility:** LinkedIn's algorithms favor complete profiles, making you more likely to appear in search results.

Key Elements of an Effective LinkedIn Profile

1. Professional Headshot: Your profile picture should be clear, professional, and friendly. According to LinkedIn, profiles with a photo get up to 21 times more views and up to 36 times more messages.

2. Compelling Headline: Your headline, which appears under your name, should include your job title and a value proposition if possible. It's one of the first things people see, so make it count.

3. Detailed Summary: The summary section is your chance to tell your professional story. Highlight your skills, experience, and what you bring to the table.

4. Experience Section: List your current position and at least two past positions. Be sure to include accomplishments, not just duties.

5. Skills & Endorsements: List your most relevant skills. Endorsements from your connections can add credibility.

6. Recommendations: These serve as testimonials on your profile. Don't hesitate to ask colleagues or clients for recommendations.

7. Education & Certifications: Include any degrees or certifications that add value to your professional persona.

8. Contact Information: Make sure your contact information is up-to-date and that people know the best way to reach you.

By carefully optimizing your LinkedIn profile, you're not just making a good first impression. You're building the foundation of your personal brand on the platform, and that can make a big difference in your LinkedIn marketing efforts. In the next chapter, we'll dive into the world of InMails and how to use them effectively for prospecting.

Chapter 10: Social Selling and Success with Sales Navigator

In the digital age, selling has evolved to accommodate the new ways in which people interact and communicate. Social selling, which leverages social networks to find, connect with, understand, and nurture sales prospects, is becoming an increasingly important part of this evolution. In this chapter, we'll explore the impact of social selling and how you can use LinkedIn Sales Navigator to elevate your social selling game.

The Impact of Social Selling

Social selling is about building relationships and trust by offering value to your prospects. Here's why it's crucial:

- **Builds Trust and Credibility:** By sharing relevant content, commenting on news, and reaching out directly to answer questions, you can build a reputation as a helpful, knowledgeable resource.

- **Fosters Long-term Relationships:** Social selling is not about instant sales. Instead, it's about building deep relationships that can lead to ongoing business and referrals.

- **Creates a Personal Brand:** Social selling allows you to showcase your expertise, establishing you as a thought leader in your industry.

- **Better Understanding of Prospects:** Social media gives you insight into what your prospects care about, their pain points, and their needs.

This understanding can inform your sales approach.

Using Sales Navigator to Increase Win Rates and Deal Sizes

LinkedIn Sales Navigator is a powerful tool for social selling. It can help you find the right prospects, understand what they value, and engage with them effectively. Here's how:

- **Find the Right Prospects:** Sales Navigator's advanced search and lead recommendation features help you find the right people faster.

- **Understand Key Insights:** Stay informed with timely and relevant insights about your prospects and accounts.

- Engage Effectively: Reach out directly with personalized outreach using InMail, or engage with prospects' content to get on their radar.

- Stay Organized: With lead and account management features, you can keep track of your prospects, your interactions, and your progress.

By incorporating LinkedIn Sales Navigator into your social selling strategy, you can increase win rates and deal sizes, according to LinkedIn data. As you continue to use the platform, you'll find that it becomes an indispensable tool for building relationships, understanding your prospects, and ultimately, achieving your sales goals.

11. Conclusion

As we reach the end of this guide, it's time to look forward to the future of LinkedIn Marketing and Sales Navigator. We also underscore the importance of staying abreast with the constant changes and enhancements that LinkedIn introduces to better serve its users.

The Future of LinkedIn Marketing and Sales Navigator

The digital landscape is ever-evolving, and LinkedIn is no exception. As we look towards the future, LinkedIn is likely to continue enhancing its features and tools to create a more personalized and effective platform for businesses.

LinkedIn's recent updates and new features suggest a future where data-driven insights and artificial intelligence play a significant role in refining user experience and delivering more precise, actionable results.

Sales Navigator, too, is expected to evolve, becoming an even more powerful tool for social selling. We anticipate more granular search features, better integration with other digital tools, and enhanced capabilities for tracking and managing leads and accounts.

Staying Updated with LinkedIn's Changes and Enhancements

As LinkedIn continues to evolve, it's crucial to stay informed about its latest changes and enhancements. Here's how:

- **Follow LinkedIn's Official Blog:** LinkedIn regularly posts updates, news, and tips on their official blog.

- **Subscribe to Newsletters:** Many digital marketing blogs and websites offer newsletters that keep you informed about the latest changes in social media platforms, including LinkedIn.

- **Participate in LinkedIn Groups:** Join LinkedIn groups that focus on LinkedIn marketing. These groups often share news, tips, and best practices.

- **Attend LinkedIn Events/Webinars:** LinkedIn and other organizations often hold events or webinars when major updates are launched.

These sessions can provide deeper insights into new features and how to use them effectively.

As we conclude, remember that success in LinkedIn marketing does not happen overnight. It's a gradual process of building your profile, connecting with the right people, delivering valuable content, and leveraging tools like Sales Navigator to find, understand, and engage with prospects.

By consistently applying the principles and strategies outlined in this guide, you will be well on your way to becoming a LinkedIn marketing pro. Here's to your success with LinkedIn Marketing and Sales Navigator!

Dear Reader,

First and foremost, thank you. Whether you are a seasoned professional seeking to refine your LinkedIn strategy or a beginner setting foot into the realm of LinkedIn marketing, your willingness to learn and grow is commendable. I am sincerely grateful for your trust in this guide as a stepping stone on your journey to mastering LinkedIn Marketing.

As the CEO of CalculatedLeads.com, I understand the challenges and rewards of navigating the digital marketing landscape. The lessons shared in this book are a culmination of my experiences, mistakes, and successes.

My hope is that they provide you with valuable insights and practical tools to effectively leverage LinkedIn Sales Navigator to amplify your business and generate organic leads.

I believe in the power of learning, and I am committed to continuing this journey of knowledge with you. I invite you to visit our website, CalculatedLeads.com, for more resources and insights into digital marketing strategies. You can also reach out to me directly on LinkedIn – I always appreciate connecting with readers and learning from their experiences.

Remember, the journey to becoming a LinkedIn marketing pro is a marathon, not a sprint.

Patience, persistence, and a willingness to learn will be your greatest allies.

Again, thank you for embarking on this journey with me. I wish you every success in your LinkedIn marketing endeavors.

Warm regards,

Joel Erlichson CEO,
CalculatedLeads.com
Author, "LinkedIn Marketing: How To Amplify Your Business and Generate Organic Leads with Sales Navigator"

Thank You

Made in the USA
Columbia, SC
22 October 2023